Every show get crazy and crazy

We growing and growing every, every,

VOICES IN HIP-HOP / MIGOS

Takeoff, Quavo, and Offset

VOICES IN HIP-HOP

MIGOS

MAXX FIDALGO

CREATIVE EDUCATION / CREATIVE PAPERBACKS

Dropped out

didn't gradu

But I s

my pla

Mama

good j

Published by Creative Education and Creative Paperbacks
P.O. Box 227, Mankato, Minnesota 56002
Creative Education and Creative Paperbacks are imprints of The Creative Company
www.thecreativecompany.us

Design by Graham Morgan
Art direction by Blue Design (www.bluedes.com)

Images by Getty Images/Aaron J. Thornton, 18–19, Brad Barket, 12, Christopher Polk, 4, 40, David Becker, 27, 38, David Wolff - Patrick, 23, 28, Johnny Nunez, 16, Jon Kopaloff, 2, Joseph Okpako, 24, Manny Carabel, 9, Marcus Ingram, 14, 32, MICHAEL TRAN, 10, Paras Griffin, 36–37; Wikimedia Commons/Jørund Føreland Pedersen, cover, 3, The Come Up Show, 42
Every effort has been made to contact copyright holders for material reproduced in this book. Any omissions will be rectified in subsequent printings if notice is given to the publisher.

Library of Congress Cataloging-in-Publication Data
Names: Fidalgo, Maxx, author.
Title: Migos / by Maxx Fidalgo.
Description: Mankato, Minnesota : Creative Education and Creative Paperbacks, 2026. | Series: Voices in hip-hop | Includes index. | Audience: Ages 12–15 | Audience: Grades 7–9 | Summary: "Listen up! It's Migos, the energetic, rapid-fire hip-hop group. Part biography, part song lyric collection, this music-fueled title for high school readers celebrates the rap group's journey and voice. Includes a selected discography and index"– Provided by publisher.
Identifiers: LCCN 2024055845 (print) | LCCN 2024055846 (ebook) | ISBN 9798889892816 (library binding) | ISBN 9781682776476 (paperback) | ISBN 9798889893929 (ebook)
Subjects: LCSH: Migos (Musical group)–Juvenile literature.
Classification: LCC ML3930.M624 F54 2026 (print) | LCC ML3930.M624 (ebook) | DDC 782.421649092/2 [B]–dc23/eng/20241120
LC record available at https://lccn.loc.gov/2024055845
LC ebook record available at https://lccn.loc.gov/2024055846

Printed in India

of school I

te (Oh no)

the M’s on

, oh yeah)

eally have a

, no, mama)

contents

Foreword 8

Introduction 11

Before They Were Migos 13

Learning on Their Feet 15

Breaking Out 18

'Bad and Boujee' Big Break 22

In the Limelight 26

The 'Migos Flow' 29

Making Trap Music 31

The Migos Invasion 34

Can't Outrun the Past 39

Standing with Their Communities 41

The End of an Era 45

Selected Works by Migos 47

Index 48

Foreword

"I'd like to thank the Migos—not for being on the show, but for making 'Bad and Boujee.'

"I think that they're the Beatles of this generation, and they don't get a lot of respect, I think, outside of Atlanta. Not that they don't get respect, but there's a generation, sort of like the YouTube generation that I kind of came up with. There's a generation of kids that are growing up on something that's completely separate from a whole group of people.

"Honestly, that song is just fly."

—RAPPER, ACTOR, AND PRODUCER DONALD GLOVER, ALSO KNOWN AS "CHILDISH GAMBINO," IN HIS 2017 GOLDEN GLOBES BEST COMEDY SERIES WIN ACCEPTANCE SPEECH

Offset

Quavo

Introduction

• • •

One of the biggest influences on hip-hop throughout the 2010s was Migos, a group from North Atlanta, Georgia. Migos popularized a rap style known as the "triplet flow" and a dance called the "dab." Talked up by great musicians like Drake and international music publications like *Billboard*, it's no wonder their fast, bright, fun sound caused rapper and fellow Atlantan Donald Glover, also known by his stage name Childish Gambino, to describe them as "the Beatles of our generation." Just like the Beatles "invaded" the United States and rock in the 1960s, Migos invaded 21st-century rap. They spread the sub-genre of trap music (so named for houses where drugs were made) into today's hip-hop and rap scene. Years later, Migos' sound is still heard in three-beat rhythms and rhymes throughout the music scene as a staple technique.

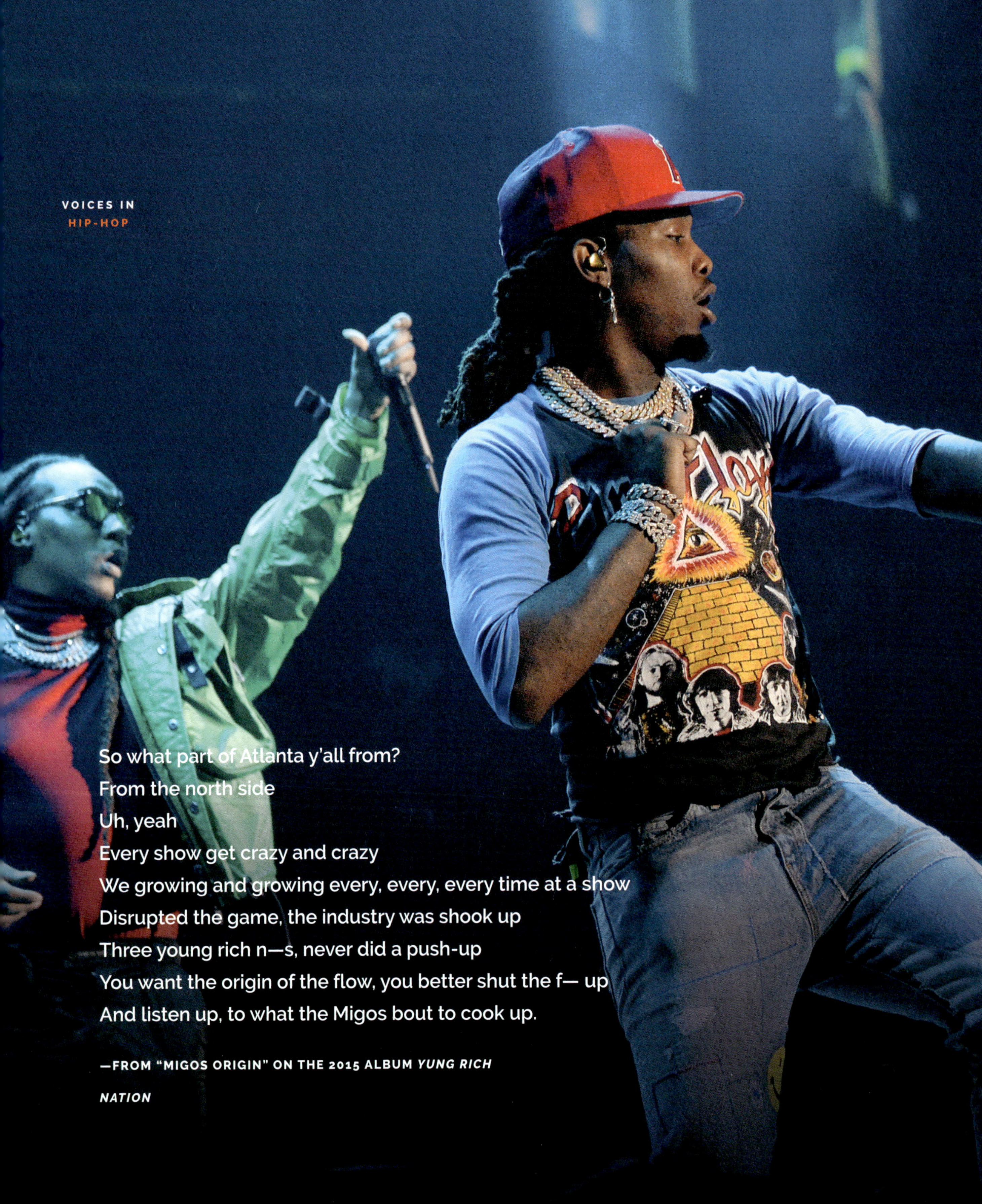

So what part of Atlanta y'all from?
From the north side
Uh, yeah
Every show get crazy and crazy
We growing and growing every, every, every time at a show
Disrupted the game, the industry was shook up
Three young rich n—s, never did a push-up
You want the origin of the flow, you better shut the f— up
And listen up, to what the Migos bout to cook up.

—FROM "MIGOS ORIGIN" ON THE 2015 ALBUM *YUNG RICH NATION*

Migos performing in Newark, New Jersey, in 2019

Before They Were Migos

• • •

Before they were Migos, they were three brothers from Gwinnett County, Georgia. Musicians Quavo, Offset, and Takeoff were born Quavious Marshall, Kiari Cyphus, and Kirshnik Ball. The three young Black men were raised by Quavo's mother, Edna Marshall, in Lawrenceville, a neighborhood of North Atlanta. Although she was "Mama" to all three, only Quavo is her biological son. Takeoff was actually her grandson and Quavo's nephew, born to Quavo's sister Titania Davenport-Treet. While loyalty made them family, Offset was not related to either Quavo or Takeoff by birth. But with the trio Migos, a short version of the Spanish word *amigos,* friends were just as close and important as family.

"The Nawfside" of Atlanta was not always an easy place to live, though Migos loved their hometown. Drugs and violence were never far, and their "beat" often caught the ear of young people in need of money. Migos were no exception. There was, after all, only one parent figure to provide for them. Money could be hard to hold onto for Mama with three growing kids. She watched out for them and wanted to keep them safe, but Quavious, Kiari, and Kirshnik wanted to help her out, too. So, the boys took to the streets often. They made ends meet by taking jobs that occasionally got them in trouble with the police.

Mama told me (Ayy)
Not to sell work (Mama)
Seventeen five, same color T-shirt (White)
(...)
I'ma get that bag, n—, ain't no doubt about it (Yup)
I'ma feed my family, n—, ain't no way around it (Family)
Ain't gon' never let up, n—, God said show my talent (Show it)
Young n— with the Anna, walkin' with the hammer (Grrah)
Talkin' country grammar, n—, straight out Nawf Atlanta (Nawfside)

—FROM "T-SHIRT" ON THE 2017 ALBUM *CULTURE*

Quavo

Learning on Their Feet

From their earliest days, Migos showed they weren't interested in an average life. Quavo made it to his senior year of high school before dropping out. Though he struggled with academics, he did love football and was the starting quarterback on his high school team his senior year. But his love of sports wasn't stronger than his love for creativity and music, and he made the risky decision to leave school. In his younger years, Offset was a dancer for musicians Whitney Houston and TLC. His earliest brush with fame didn't last. Offset was kicked out of most schools in the area for fighting; his wild spirit couldn't be ruled. Takeoff would rather be collecting backing beats than doing school work. The boys struggled against, and rejected, a traditional

Offset, Takeoff, and Quavo

lifestyle, fueled by the passion they had for making music. By 2011, their last, pre-fame run-in with the law finally convinced them it was time for a change.

One thing they loved doing for fun that kept them out of trouble was rapping. Growing up close gave them the advantage of familiarity—each one knew their two group mates well. This led to their ability to have great flow with their rapping over their backing beats, since they could anticipate one another's themes and timing. They practiced, making music together often. They made up the nicknames Quavo, Offset, and Takeoff.

Their tools weren't all that mighty to start. They had only their ability to write music, influenced by artists such as Lil Wayne, Soulja Boy, and Master P. Like their favorite rappers before them, Migos chose to pull from their lived experiences and background. Takeoff's collection of ripped backing beats became the melody they put words to. Eventually, they saved enough money to buy recording equipment. Mama's basement became their first studio.

Dropped out of school I didn't graduate (Oh no)
But I still got the M's on my plate (Oh, oh yeah)
Mama ain't really have a good job (Oh, no, mama)
But now she ain't never gotta have no job (No, no)
'Cause I work hard for mine yeah (Work hard)

—FROM "WORK HARD" ON THE 2018 ALBUM *CULTURE II*

Breaking Out

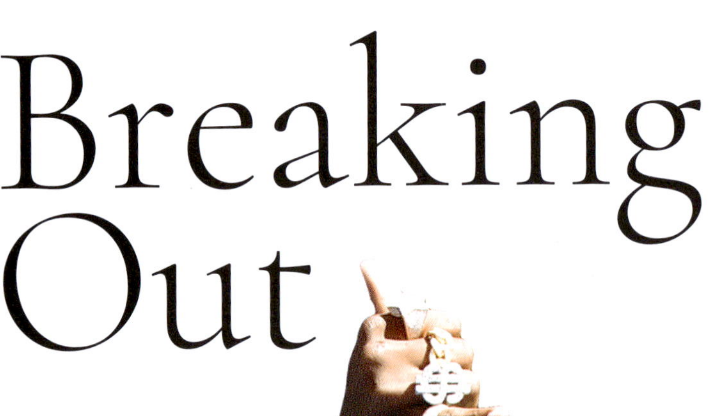

In the 15 years they were active (2008–2023, officially), Migos would release no fewer than 21 bodies of musical work, including mixtapes, studio albums, extended plays, and compilation albums made with multiple artists. However, only a handful of these works are well known, featuring their top songs.

Migos made their breakout mixtape *Y.R.N.* (*Young Rich N—s*) in 2013. That was the year their first hit, "Versace," rolled into mainstream culture, raised up by its remixing by Drake.

Drake's remix gave Migos the leg up they needed. It was the fastest way to make it without being on a big label. Like their role model Lil

Offset, Takeoff, and Quavo

. . . Heard you livi
in a mansion
in all your
raps, though

. . . But your s—
look like the

Wayne, Migos wanted to be independent. This meant they weren't having their music produced by a big record company. Since they weren't with a big company, it was a big deal that Drake, who was with a big company, found their song. His remix gave Migos their first real taste of superstar fame and attention.

From there, it took two full years for Migos to release their first studio album, *Yung Rich Nation,* in 2015. Though *Yung Rich Nation* featured platinum artist Chris Brown, the album didn't produce any top songs.

It would take another two years for Migos to produce an album that included a major hit. That album was the 2017 *Culture,* which featured the famous "Bad and Boujee." Though "Versace" had put Migos on the map, it was "Bad and Boujee" that catapulted them to stardom.

Heard you livin' in a mansion in all your raps, though
But your s— look like the trap on this Google Maps, though
We been brothers since Versace bando, whoa
Name ringin' like a Migo trap phone, whoa
Used to be with Vashtie at Santo's
That's on Tommy Campos, we live like Sopranos and I—
Walk it like I talk it (Walk it)

—FROM "WALK IT TALK IT" ON THE 2018 ALBUM *CULTURE II*

VOICES IN
HIP-HOP

'Bad and Boujee' Big Break

• • •

Migos were not supposed to be in the song "Bad and Boujee" at all. On a last-minute whim, rapper Lil Uzi, who the song was written for, decided to include his friends. In an excited rush, Quavo—known as the quick lyricist—jumped in. Offset, pulling from the local slang where they grew up, laid it on thick with "boujee." Boujee is slang for the French word bourgeois, which describes

Offset, Quavo, and Takeoff

Migos performing in London, United Kingdom, in 2021

upper-middle class people obsessed with material things that show their wealth. In a rush, Migos applied their hard work and specific talents to the song, just as they had on their own mixtapes when they were just starting out.

Offset used boujee to describe a romantic partner who liked expensive things. As Migos grew their fame, they also grew their bank accounts. Now they could afford to be with someone who liked expensive things, and they could buy those things, too. Migos had come from hard times, done hard work, and made it big where they could play just as hard. In a 2017 interview with *Complex,* Takeoff explained: "It's not about how people take what we're saying. It's more about what 'Bad and Boujee' means to us, our story, and our journey."

Their next boost up the ladder of fame was given by Glover. Glover was also from Atlanta and connected to the music community there. That's where he met Migos. In 2017, he asked Migos to be on his TV show *Atlanta* because he loved their sound. When Glover won a Golden Globe television award for the show that year, he thanked many people, including Migos. On that international stage, comparing Migos to the Beatles and naming "Bad and Boujee" as the best song, he helped the world learn about Migos's music on a large scale.

Once people took to their social media and the internet to learn about Migos, the trio's natural talent did the rest. They performed on late-night shows, on tour, and in interviews. "Bad and Boujee" came in at number one on the Billboard Hot 100 for three weeks in a row. It stayed on the chart for 34 weeks in total.

In the Limelight

With the roaring success of *Culture,* Migos released its successor, *Culture II,* in 2018. They packed this album full of big names like 2 Chainz, 21 Savage, Cardi B, Drake, Gucci Mane, Kanye West, Nicki Minaj, Post Malone, and Pharrell Williams. Songs like "MotorSport," "Stir Fry," and "Walk It Talk It" all made it in the top 10 on the Billboard Hot 100. *Culture II* went where *Culture* did not—the number one spot as an album on the Billboard 200 in its first week. Later, it would be in the top 10 most popular albums of 2018.

Offset

Takeoff

The 'Migos Flow'

As more music came out, people realized the effect Migos were having. Their signature technique, the triplet flow, was picked up by other artists in hip-hop and rap. It was called the "Migos flow." Established artists Migos worked with, like Drake and Kanye West, were copying Migos. Many people see copying as a compliment. Migos saw it as going too far—they weren't getting recognition for their work. Offset said in an interview with *Billboard*: "If you go back in time and listen to music prior to 2013, the cadence and the flow didn't matter. It was more about the bars and what you're saying. Now, people get away with not saying nothing as long as the cadence and flow are good, and I feel like we created that. We did. I remember when Quavo was most influential in 2013. It just don't be no respect given, but that's how my generation is anyway."

But Migos couldn't take all the credit for the triplet flow. Music naturally has triplets—when three notes quickly happen inside one beat. With rap, a triplet flow is when three syllables are used, instead of three music notes. They happen in words and phrases and also multiple times in a verse and song. Migos were not the first rappers to use triplet flow. It was used in the early 1990s, for example, by hip-hop artists like Three 6 Mafia and Bone Thugs-N-Harmony.

However, the triplet flow was the Migos' bread and butter. Just like there were three of them, there were three beats to their flow. Migos used the technique both in their top songs and most overall, so fans and critics associated it with them the most. The more Migos used it, the more other artists wanted to use it too, hoping to reach the kind of popularity Migos had. Suddenly, hip-hop and rap were overflowing with this quick, three-based way of singing. Now, it's common in this genre.

Medusa, Medusa, Medusa
These n—s, they wishing they knew ya
They coppin' the Truey, remixing the Louie
My blunts is fat as Rasputia
In a striped shirt like I'm Tony the Tiger
I'm beating the pot, Call me Michael
Lot of you n—s they copy
Look at my closet Versace, Versace

—FROM "VERSACE" ON THE 2013 MIXTAPE *Y.R.N. (YUNG RICH N—S)*

Making Trap Music

Migos brought their local sound of North Atlanta to the rest of the world. It was loud, pumping, bright party music. They had hard and fast beats they would rap to and play off each other like a big game of ad libs set to a melody. Many times, they would use their personal life experience to create lyrics. They would sing about getting famous and bragging as in "Versace." They would sing about buying luxury cars and putting down competition as in their 2018 collaboration with Cardi B and Nicki Minaj, "MotorSport."

Takeoff

Migos were not afraid to have fun with their music. They had started rapping for fun and were keeping it that way in their professional lives. But they were also not afraid to rap about hard topics that were a reality where they grew up. Drugs, weapons, violence, racism, and sex are all topics found in their songs. Rap music with darker themes and a harsher sound is called trap, after the word for abandoned houses that are used to make and sell illegal drugs. Trap music came from the southern United States. Migos leaned into the trap sound from their home region with bops like "Walk It Talk It," even referencing the genre in the lyrics themselves. When people seemed to like that, they decided to continue borrowing from home.

TRAP MUSIC

Though versions of trap music were heard in 1990s rap and hip-hop, this sub-genre was really born in the early 2000s. The harsh drums, thumping beats, and dark lyrics were recognized and cultivated by music producer Shawty Redd. The sub-genre came out most famously from artists from Atlanta. They included three artists who brought the sub-genre to the mainstream with Redd: rappers Young Jeezy, Gucci Mane, and T.I. Trap gets its name from houses in predominantly Black neighborhoods in the southern United States where drugs were made, sold, and distributed. Trap music often paints a picture of what living in poverty-stricken neighborhoods is like.

VOICES IN HIP-HOP

The Migos Invasion

The music Migos made was either high-energy and fun, or gritty and real. They gave fans something easy to listen to or another look at life with stories from their past. Terms such as "trap" and "boujee" that were popular in their communities in Atlanta were repeated on their records and made it to thousands of people's ears. Those terms became second nature in the mouths of everyday people who may have never been to Georgia. Popular dances created by unknown faces on Gwinnett County streets got pulled into Migos videos. The most popular example was the dab. Once Migos put the dance into music, younger groups of people shared it in their communities. Even famous people like football player Cam Newton and politician Hillary Clinton did the dab.

THE DAB

While Migos briefly claimed ownership of creating the dab, the dance has really been out for decades. One version was seen in Japan as early as the 1990s. The dab became popular in Black communities in the southern United States, where it could be seen since the 2000s. The dab move is done by leaning your head into one arm that is bent at a 90-degree angle and pointed up. The other arm is stuck out straight away from the body and angled up in the same direction. Celebrities, anime characters, and politicians have "dabbed."

Migos were also known for referencing pop culture. For example, they said they were like the Sopranos, a family in a TV crime drama from the early 2000s. Migos compared themselves to famous criminals like mafia boss Jon Gotti and popular figures like singer Brittney Spears. One song, "Stir Fry," dropped the name of fast-food restaurant Popeyes, which is popular in the southern United States. People could recognize the things Migos sang about, and listeners connected to the concepts. The trio's following bloomed. Memes of their music, such as the opening line of "Bad and Boujee," spread on the internet. Jokes about Migos being better than or similar to the Beatles started after Glover made the claim. Migos stayed fun, so fans stayed with Migos. It kept them relevant.

The Migos exhibit at the Trap Music Museum in Atlanta, Georgia

You don't wanna go there (Nah)
Sticks and the Dracos in here (Brrt)
Got racks in the back of my pants (Racks)
Got racks in the bachelor pad (Racks)
These b—s, they f— for a bag (Smash)
And you n—s gon' go out sad
Bad Mona Lisa (Bad), slide with my people (Skrrt skrrt)
Pink slip for the ride (Skrrt skrrt), but what's in the trunk, it's illegal
Came from dimes (Dimes), no cosigns (No cosigns)
You can read between the lines
Like a pro skater, did my own grinds, yeah (Grinds)

—FROM "WHAT THE PRICE" ON THE 2017 ALBUM *CULTURE*

Takeoff (foreground)

Can't Outrun the Past

The trouble Migos got into as young men never really left them. The first shock came when fans were stabbed at one of their concerts in 2015. The person behind the act had really wanted to hurt Migos. This threat didn't stop the group from making and performing music.

The trouble didn't stay with just zealous fans, either. Migos themselves were caught up in it, too. In 2015, during a concert at Georgia Southern University on their home turf, the three rappers were arrested. Drugs and guns were found in the vans they brought with them to the concert. Quavo and Takeoff were eventually released, but Offset was put in jail. He was the only member of Migos with an earlier history of burglary and theft. While it helped him lay down real, truthful lyrics, it also worked against him. The group was split up for eight months while Offset was in jail. More than anything, though, Migos were musicians. As he served time away from his family and group mates, Offset wrote music every day.

In 2016, Offset was arrested again. According to reports, it was because he was driving with a suspended driver's license. Offset said his license was valid, and he proved correct. He was released.

Takeoff performs during the 2018 Coachella Valley Music and Arts Festival in Indio, California.

> Got dope like Pablo (Pablo)
> Cut throat like Pablo (Cut throat)
> Chop trees with the Draco (Draco)
> On the Nawf, got Diego (Diego)
> Say "Hasta luego" (Luego)
> Muy Bien wrap a kilo (Yeah)
>
> **—FROM "NARCOS" ON THE 2018 ALBUM *CULTURE II***

Standing with Their Communities

As young Black men, Migos experienced racism first-hand. At times they were accused of crimes in the harder parts of North Atlanta. Later, the charges were dropped. The three friends have never officially said what the charges were. But

Quavo

they sing about drug-dealing and gang violence. In their song "Narcos," they portray the police in negative terms, which is at variance with the heroic image painted by others.

As superstars, Migos didn't make waves in politics or social causes very often. So when they signed a petition with other artists in 2020 to put more rules on the New York Police Department, it made waves. Along with artists like Rihanna, Meek Mills, and Megan Thee Stallion, Migos sided with many of their fans in asking for police reform. It was during the height of the Black Lives Matter movement.

BLACK LIVES MATTER

The Black Lives Matter movement was born in 2013 in response to the 2012 death of 17-year-old Trayvon Martin in Sanford, Florida, and the subsequent acquittal of his shooter, George Zimmerman. The movement seeks to fight systemic racism. Black Lives Matter reached its height in 2020, after the murder of George Floyd by Minneapolis, Minnesota, police officers. Today, Black Lives Matter is part of a global movement also recognized in countries other than the United States.

Turn a n— to a mummy with the payment (Woo, woo)
Terminate him with the money (Hey!), it was gravy (Terminator)
Spin an opp block, rock-a-bye-baby (Rock-a-bye)
Made his heart stop, made his momma hate me (Make 'em hate me)

—FROM "STRAIGHTENIN" ON THE 2021 ALBUM *CULTURE III*

Turn a n— to
mummy with
the payment
(Woo, woo)

Terminate hi
with the

The End of an Era

The COVID-19 pandemic delayed Migos' last album *Culture III*. It was the end of their *Culture* album trilogy—three for three, just like the three Migos. Though it peaked at number two on the Billboard 200 the week it was released in the United States, the album ended the year ranked at 95.

After releasing the album in 2021, Migos hit a rough patch. The members gave different reasons for their rift. Quavo said it was lack of loyalty. Takeoff, the youngest and usually quietest, supported his uncle. Offset said the musicians had decided to go in different professional directions. By mid-2022, the group that brought new phrases into everyday speech was broken up in every way except officially. Quavo and Takeoff put out a new, duo album, *Only Built for Infinity Links*, that October. Offset had his hands full with his family—wife Cardi B and his (then) five children. Then, tragedy struck.

OFFSET AND CARDI B

The relationship between Offset and another hip-hop star, Cardi B, began in early 2017. The couple were secretly married that September—in fact, before Offset publicly proposed to Cardi B at a concert in Philadelphia, Pennsylvania, that October. Cardi B filed for divorce in September 2020, but the couple reconciled just weeks later. She also filed for divorce again in the summer of 2024. The couple have repeatedly accused each other of cheating, then proclaimed their love for each other and given each other, and their children, lavish gifts. Offset and Cardi B share three children, the youngest of whom was born in September 2024. Offset also has three other children from previous relationships.

On November 1, 2022, Takeoff's life was violently taken. In the early morning, he and two acquaintances were shot. The suspect was a person they were hanging out with. Outside a Houston, Texas, bowling alley, one of the great lyricists of hip-hop took his last breath with his uncle by his side.

After the death of Takeoff, the group was officially no more. Takeoff was "the glue" that kept the group together. Without Takeoff, they weren't really Migos. Offset would go solo. Quavo would dedicate his 2023 album, *Rocket Power,* to Takeoff's memory.

Even before Takeoff was killed, Migos had been fading into the background of the music scene, shown most obviously by their split, solo careers, and long stretch of years between joint albums. Yet, their influence lives on in every catchy lyric and pop culture reference that those three boys from Lawrenceville brought to the rest of the world.

SELECTED WORKS BY MIGOS

COMPILATION ALBUMS

Quality Control: Control the Streets, Volume 2, 2019

Quality Control: Control the Streets, Volume 1, 2017

Tru Colors, 2016

EPS

3 Way, 2016

Trap Symphony, 2015

MIXTAPES

Y.R.N. 2 (Young Rich N–s 2), 2016

Rich Shooters, 2015

Streets On Lock 4, 2015

Back To The Bando, 2015

Currency, 2015

Still On Lock, 2015

Migo Lingo, 2015

*Rich N**a Timeline*, 2014

World War 3D: The Green Album, 2014

Streets On Lock 3, 2014

No Label 2, 2014

Solid Foundation, 2014

Lobby Runners, 2013

Streets On Lock 2, 2013

Streets On Lock 1, 2013

Y.R.N. (Young Rich N–s), 2013

No Label, 2012

Juug Season, 2011

STUDIO ALBUMS

Culture III, 2021

Culture II, 2018

Culture, 2017

Yung Rich Nation, 2015

INDEX

albums
Culture, 14, 21, 26, 37, 47
Culture II, 17, 21, 26, 40, 47
Culture III, 43, 45, 47
Only Built for Infinity Links, 45
Yung Rich Nation, 12, 21, 47
Atlanta (TV show), 25
Ball, Kirshnik (Takeoff's birth name), 13, 14,
Beatles, 8, 11, 25, 35
Billboard, 11, 25, 26, 29, 45
Black Lives Matter, 45
Cardi B, 26, 31, 45, 46
Childish Gambino, 8, 11, 25, 35,
Clinton, Hillary, 35
Cyphus, Kiari (Offset's birth name), 13, 14
dab, 11, 34, 35
Davenport-Treet, Titania (Quavo's sister, Takeoff's mother), 13
death of Takeoff, 46
Drake, 11, 18, 21, 26, 29
Georgia Southern University, 39
Glover, Donald. See Childish Gambino
Golden Globes, 8, 25
Gwinnett County, Georgia, 13, 34
legal troubles, 14, 17, 39–40, 41
Lil Uzi, 22
Lil Wayne, 17, 18, 21
Marshall, Edna (Quavo's mother), 13
Marshall, Quavious (Quavo's birth name)
Migos flow, 29–30
mixtape
Y.R.N. (Young Rich N—s), 18, 30, 47
Newton, Cam, 35
North Atlanta, Georgia, 11, 12, 13, 31, 41
Rocket Power (album by Takeoff), 46
Shawty Redd, 33
songs
"Bad and Boujee," 8, 21, 22–25, 35
"Migos Origin," 12
"MotorSport," 26, 31
"Narcos," 40, 43
"Stir Fry," 26, 35
"Straightenin," 43
"T-shirt," 14
"Versace," 18, 21, 30, 31
"Walk It Talk It," 21, 26, 33
"What the Price," 37
"Work Hard," 17
Sopranos (fictional crime family), 21, 35
trap music, 11, 31–33, 34, 36,
triplet flow, 11, 29–30
West, Kanye, 26, 29